Spring
on the farm

by Jillian Powell

Wayland
HODDER

an imprint of Hodder Children's Books

Titles in the series

Summer on the farm
Autumn on the farm
Winter on the farm
Spring on the farm

Picture Acknowledgements

The publishers would like to thank the following for allowing their photographs to be reproduced in this book:
Agripicture/Peter Dean 6 inset, 12, 13, 14, 15, 16 top, 19, 22 bottom, 23; Cephas 5 top (D.K. M. Photo), 6 top (Fred R. Palmer), 10 (Mick Rock); Bruce Coleman Ltd 27 inset (J. Brackenbury); Frank Lane Picture Agency 5 bottom (Roger Wilmshurst), 7 (Eric and David Hoskin), 17 top (Peter Reynold[...] Marque 17 (bottom);Natural History Photographic Agency 26 (Jane Gifford[...]ord Scientific Films 16 bottom (Rainer Berg/Okapia), 24, 25 (Doug Allen); Still[...]T.B.); Tony Stone Worldwide front cover (Simon Jauncey), 11 (David Woodfall),[...]7 top, 28 bottom (Janerik Henriksson);

Series editors: Francesca Motisi and Sarah Doughty
Book editor: Joan Walters
Series and book designer: Jean Wheeler

First published in 1996 by
Wayland (Publishers) Limited
This paperback edition published in 2001 by Hodder Wayland,
an imprint of Hodder Children's Books

© Hodder Wayland 1996

British Library Cataloguing in Publication Data

Powell, Jillian
Spring on the farm. - (The farming year)
1. Agriculture - Juvenile literature 2. Spring - Juvenile literature
I. Title II. Series
630

ISBN 0-7502-3430-X

Typeset by Jean Wheeler
Printed and bound by G. Canale and C.S.p.A., Turin, Italy

Contents

Introduction

Spring is a busy time on the farm. After the cold winter months, the weather starts to get warmer. Trees and plants which lost their leaves in winter start to grow again. Plants grow fastest in the spring.

The warmth of the sun and the rainy spring days help new plants grow. Now is the time for the farmer to sow seeds for crops of maize, spring wheat and barley.

Spring is also the time when many farm animals, such as sheep and cows, have their babies. Sheep give birth to lambs and cows give birth to calves.

Getting ready for planting

The farmer uses a tractor with special tools to get the fields ready for the new crops. Before the seeds can be sown, the fields must be ploughed. Ploughing the earth kills weeds and helps air and water spread through the soil. This makes it easier for the crops to grow. The plough has big metal blades which break up and turn over the earth.

When the field has been ploughed,
the farmer fixes a harrow to the
tractor. A harrow is like a huge rake
which breaks up the big slices of
earth made by the plough.

The tractor above pulls a big roller over
the earth to make it flat again. Now the
field is ready for seeds to be planted.

Using a seed drill

In spring, the farmer plants crops such as spring wheat, spring barley and maize. The seeds are sown in rows so all the plants can get the light, food and water which they need to grow.

The tractor pulls a tool called a seed drill. The seeds are carried in a box at the back called a seed hopper.

The seed drill rakes neat rows in the earth and drops the seeds down into the rows. The spikes on the drill cover the seeds with earth so they will be able to grow. As the seed drill sows the seeds, it drops some fertilizer on to the earth. Rain will help the seeds to start growing.

Keeping crops healthy

Crops which were sown in the autumn are growing well by now. You may see fields of oil seed rape which has bright yellow flowers. The seeds are used to make cooking oil, margarine and other foods.

All plants need food, especially in the spring
when they are growing fast. Some farmers
spray crops with fertilizer to help them grow.
They may also spray crops with chemicals
which kill insects, weeds and diseases.

Planting potatoes

As the weather gets warmer, there are no more frosty nights. Frost can kill young plants. Now the farmer can plant crops, such as potatoes. First, the tractor pulls a special machine over the fields which takes stones out of the earth. Stones could spoil potatoes when they are being harvested.

A machine called a potato planter plants the seed potatoes. The machine carries the seed potatoes in a box at the back. As the tractor moves forward the potatoes fall out in rows into the earth. The big teeth on the machine cover the potatoes with earth.

Making silage

The warm, wet spring weather helps grass to start growing again. Soon there will be plenty of fresh grass for farm animals to feed on. Even now, the farmer must think ahead to the winter months when the grass will stop growing. The farmer cuts grass to make silage to feed the farm animals in winter. Making silage is a way of keeping cut grass as juicy as possible.

A machine called a forage harvester cuts and gathers up the grass. It chops it up and blows it into a trailer.

The chopped up grass is then wrapped in black plastic so no air or light can get in. Inside, the grass turns into silage.

Dairy farming

Cattle have spent the winter months in covered yards and sheds. In spring, the farmer brings them out to graze on the fresh grass. A cow begins to make milk when she has had a calf.

Cows are milked twice a day by special machines which squeeze the milk from their udders.

The milking parlour must be kept very clean so germs cannot get into the milk. After milking is over, the parlour is washed down.

The milk is pumped into a big tank which keeps it cool. Once a day, a tanker arrives at the farm to collect the milk.

Spring calves

Some calves are born in the spring.
A cow usually has her first calf when
she is about two years old. On a farm
where cattle are kept for beef, the calves
feed on their mothers' milk. They wear
tags in their ears so the farmer can
watch how well they grow.

On a dairy farm, calves are fed on their mothers' milk for only a few days. Then the farmer feeds them on dried milk until they can eat hay, silage and fresh grass.

Some farmers keep deer for their meat, which is called venison.

The deer may live indoors in the cold winter months and in the spring they come out to graze on fresh grass.

In the late spring, the female deer
give birth to calves. The farmer
weighs each calf and puts a tag in its
ear. The calves drink their mothers'
milk until they are old enough to
graze on fresh grass.

The sheep farm

Spring is the time when most lambs are born. Female sheep are called ewes. Some farmers bring the ewes into sheds to have their lambs. The farmer feeds the ewes on hay and silage.

The lambs drink their mothers' milk which helps them grow strong and healthy.

As the weather gets warmer, the ewes can go outside to graze on fresh grass.

In spring, salmon which live wild in rivers swim out to sea. They stay in the sea for a year or more until they swim back to their home rivers to lay their eggs.

The salmon farmer copies nature. In spring, the farmer moves the young salmon from big tanks of water on the salmon farm to pens of seawater.

The salmon can swim around in the seawater inside huge nets ten metres deep. They grow for another year until they are big enough to eat.

The salmon farmer feeds them on fish food which has all the goodness they need.

The fruit farm

In spring, the trees on the fruit farm
are covered with blossom. The trees
can only make fruits if pollen is
carried from one flower to another.
This is called pollination.

The fruit farmer needs bees to pollinate the flowers. On a dry spring day a beekeeper visits the farm with hives of bees which are placed near the fruit trees.

The bees fly from flower to flower to gather sweet nectar which they will make into honey. As they visit each flower, pollen sticks to their legs and bodies.

When they visit the next flower, the pollen rubs off their bodies and sticks to the female part of the flower. This pollinates the flower so it can grow into a fruit.

Spring chicks

Spring is a time for birds to lay eggs. When a hen mates with a male bird, called a cockerel, she lays eggs that will hatch into chicks.

Hens that are kept indoors lay eggs all year round. The electric lighting makes them think that it is always springtime. The eggs are hatched in special machines which are kept as warm as a hen's body. After hatching, the chicks live and grow together in special conditions indoors.

This hen and her young are free-range chickens, which means they spend their days outside. They start having their chicks in the spring. Chicks remind us that spring is here, with all the new life the season brings.

The farming year calendar

Spring

Sowing crops for summer and autumn harvest

Harvesting vegetables grown through the winter

Fertilizing and spraying crops against weeds and diseases

Lambing

Putting animals out to graze

Silage making

Summer

Harvesting vegetables and soft fruits

Watering crops

Haymaking

Silage making

Sheep shearing and sheep dipping

Harvesting crops such as wheat and barley

Autumn

Ploughing fields after
    harvest
Sowing winter wheat
    and barley
Harvesting fruits such as
    apples and pears
Harvesting potatoes and
    sugar beet
Autumn calving
Hedge trimming

Winter

Clearing and draining
    ditches
Pruning fruit trees
Housing animals
Early indoor lambing
Fertilizing crops
Repairing farm
    buildings, fences
    and machinery

Glossary

Chemicals Sprays and powders used by farmers to keep their crops healthy.

Diseases Illnesses that can kill plants and animals.

Germs Tiny living things that can make us ill.

Harvested Crops that have been cut and gathered in.

Mates Joins together with another animal to have babies.

Milking parlour A farm building where cows are taken to be milked.

Nectar A sweet liquid made by flowers.

Plough To turn the earth over with a metal tool called a plough.

Pollen The yellow powdery grains made by flowers.

Silage Grass that has been cut and wrapped in black plastic to keep it juicy.

Tanker A truck with a big tank on the back for carrying liquids such as milk.

Udder The part of a female cow which holds her milk.

Books to read

Farming, Sue Hadden (Wayland, 1991)

Farming, Ruth Thomson (Watts, 1994)

Let's Visit a Farm series, Sarah Doughty and Diana Bentley (Wayland, 1989-90)

Index